GRIEVING
HOPE
JOY

One man's Sojourn from the deepest pits
of despair to the pinnacle of pure joy

BILL STOKES

SAGE OF THE AGE

PUBLICATION
CONSULTANTS
We Believe In The Power Of Authors

PO Box 221974 Anchorage, Alaska 99522-1974
books@publicationconsultants.com—www.publicationconsultants.com

ISBN 978-1-59433-820-5
eBook ISBN 978-1-59433-821-2
Library of Congress Catalog Card Number: 2018955758

DEDICATION

Grieving—Hope—Joy is dedicated to all who are hurting, suffering, or have pain of any kind. It is my hope that my book of poems will help them conquer the glacier of grief and find the same joy I experienced.

GRIEVING

ALONE

After all this time climbing out of
every crevasse that into
I fell to the bottom of like a stone
And despite my longing heart I know I will
be forever in the dark, dancing alone.

Alone is a terrible word that innocently condemns
for the crime of wanting all those things you lost
when your heart was from you so brutally torn
But to risk it all is so very hard to do if the
only reward will be laughter and scorn.

At the wrong end of life to put your heart on the line
For it takes an eternity to heal if rejected
and your time left is so very short in life's
hourglass that has speeding sand so fine.

After all this time climbing out of
every crevasse that into
I fell to the bottom of like a stone.
And despite my longing heart I know will
be forever in the dark, dancing alone.

Glacier of Grieving

Having to cross the glacier of grieving
is a terrifying place to be
Because with every step you risk falling into the deepest
crevasses of despair you will ever know or see.

When the love of your life is suddenly ripped away
Instantly your soul is in the deepest, coldest crevasse
there is and you must choose to either go or stay.

To stay is to bury your soul in this cruel bitter
place and abandon the light of day.
To go means that you must scream, claw and scratch
yourself up and out of this terrible abyss the entire way.

With bloody fingers and an exhausted soul
you take a weary step, perhaps two,
And again into another crevasse you break through.

As weariness and bitter sorrow tries to freeze you in
You must choose to either surrender or
fight for your life yet once again.

You must cross this glacier no matter how many
times into the crevasses of despair you do slide.
For your only salvation, and to find those you love,
is to climb up the rocky cliffs on the other side.

It is the cruelest and hardest journey you will ever make
But if you carefully choose, there are those with the
light of Christ shining from their very souls that will
light the way and with you will every step take.

Having to cross the glacier of grieving
is a terrifying place to be
Because with every step you risk falling into the deepest
crevasses of despair you will ever know or see.

CONFIDE

All of the pure jaw-clinching poems trapped on a
runaway rollercoaster ride that is now like broken
fingernails slowing carving shrill gouges down a
chalk board and you are no longer trapped inside.
And no matter where you look there are no shining
souls of pure light that you would even dare to bare
your soul and with no shame, all your fears do confide.

The words on the lines are naught but the
individual reflections of mirror shards
Of the emotions that volcanically erupt like
Krakatau that rents asunder your so very
fragile and newly-made house of cards.

Even though every day is supposed to be brand new
But when you never sleep
The days blend into a foul-smelling
and impalpable witches brew.

All of the gritty jaw-clinching poems trapped on a
runaway rollercoaster ride that is now like broken
fingernails slowing carving shrill gouges down a
chalk board and you are no longer trapped inside.
And no matter where you look there are no shining souls
of pure light that you would even dare to bare your
soul and with no shame, and all your fears do confide.

MARK

All alone in the dark
With the smell of ashes all around you
as they fall on the bed and leave their mark.

The shivering cold of being so
very alone and utterly lost
The bitter anguish that taunts your soul
and does not care about the cost.

Time on the bedroom clock
Goes by as if it were a slow motion tick
with an eon passing before the tock.

No matter how hard you try
Your eyes are never dry when your soul
knows nothing but how to cry.

All alone in the dark
With the smell of ashes all around you
as they fall on the bed and leave their mark.

Armor

An armor plated heart is such a heavy stone
It lies to you and says you are better off alone.

It traps the light of your soul behind a stony wall
And it forbids your heart into love again to ever fall.

The fragile crystal lattice of love cannot
find a single bridge support
And it shatters into a million razor sharp
shards as it falls with a sad sighing retort.

An armor plated heart is such a heavy stone
It lies to you and says you are better off alone.

Out

Like the salmon that made it to the very end of the route
Milling around, until life can no
longer stay, spawned out.

Accomplishing all of tasks of life that
allowed the perilous return to home
And at the end, there is only you in
the tiny pool so very alone.

Once a mighty King that had no fear
And now nothing but living decay and the
returning back to the elements so very near.

Like the salmon that made it to the very end of the route
Milling around, until life can no
longer stay, spawned out.

Quicksand

Like the cat, on my feet I try to so very hard to land
But every time I stumble and fall it is into quicksand.

The more you fight and struggle to get free
The deeper you go and soon sand is all that you can see.

In the dark mire you are immobile and
trapped in this sandy mote
There is a way out and you only need to
quit struggling and learn to float.

It takes courage and strength of will
And with careful choices the way out will itself reveal.

Like the cat, on my feet I try to so very hard to land
But every time I stumble and fall it is into quicksand.

ALL

You toil, work, and then you remember
and yet again tumble into free fall
The good days, the bad days, the successes, the
things that fail and when you get home, to an empty
house, only the ears on the walls hear it all.

The echo of your own voice cannot
drown out the sound of still alone
And no matter where you turn, the only things
that you can really hear are the after tones.

You toil, work, and then you remember
and yet again tumble into free fall
The good days, the bad days, the successes, the
things that fail and when you get home, to an empty
house, only the ears on the walls hear it all.

CALL

When losing everything at finding someone to truly love
And your heart is plummeting into free fall
Who do you call?

The agony of trashed dreams
Makes your already fragile heart writhe
with torture and almost muted screams.

The pure horror of facing each day so very alone
Turns your heart into a brittle flinty stone.

No emotion do you dare show
A machine you would become because
a machine does not need love
and the pain that love does grow.

Bitterness is a companion that does not
care who knows and why it is there
And would protect your heart from ever
opening up enough to allow a rip or tear.

When losing everything at finding someone to truly love
And your heart is plummeting in free fall
Who do you call?

CARE

When like mirror shards your heart and
soul seems shattered beyond repair
Is when you feel like it is already dead and you are
at death's gate and you really just don't care.

Life has a death blow dealt to you
And it seems there is no one or place of refuge to turn to.

A broken heart and contrite spirit are the keys
Our Lord and Savior's unending love for us is all we
need to see if we but get down to pray on our knees.

Mercy kind and mercy sweet
Are the fruits of forgiveness our
Lord and Savior does entreat.

There is no way out of perdition's hell
if death snared us as we fell
But the mercy of love both here and there can
give you the reason your story to others tell.

When like mirror shards your heart and
soul seems shattered beyond repair
Is when you feel like it is already dead and you are
at death's gate and you really just don't care.

CALL

First spring, first summer, first fall
Without hearing once my love's laughing call.

Watching the fireweed bloom just so
Fiery bright right to the last blossom it does go.

The days of this spring's loss
Have turned into seasons of
tumultuous time hurried toss.

Time may heal all wounds as time goes by
But it is so very hard to keep focused on
the light from a bright blue sky.

First spring, first summer, first fall
Without hearing once, my love's laughing call.

Heart

The bitter, bitter dregs of being so very alone
where there is no one who's love you are part
Does create the perfect storm for a foolish heart.

The merest chance of finding someone
who with you their soul would share
Creates wild expectations, that have no
chance of ever really being there.

A gentle kiss with love through and through
That is forever beyond your reach no matter how
much your heart begs for it to come true.

The bitter, bitter dregs of being so very alone
where there is no one who's love you are part
Does create the perfect storm for a foolish heart.

EMBERS

The fire is almost out and the flame
is now so tiny and slender
And like so many dreams, that are
now naught but embers

When we were young and so very much alive
Such grand plans we all made of the places we
would go, and where we would live out our lives.

Then real life barges in and takes its toll
And all of those dreams became
fairy tales written by trolls.

You must pick those dreams that mean the most
And get them done before your dreams
all become a hollow boast.

The fire is almost out and the flame
is now so tiny and slender
And like so many dreams, that are
now naught but embers.

Steps

When you first venture out from the
prison of despair's frozen steppes
You have to take baby steps.

So very unsure of what to say and do
And having no clue as to when or who.

There are so many risks yet unnamed
And worrying that your heart's gut wrenching weary
ache will never be fully tamed.

To give your soul to another soul
Must be the absolute goal.

Part time love never can last the test
of time's tempest tossed
For only in each other can you weather
any storm, uncaring about the cost.

When you first venture out from the
prison of despair's frozen steppes
You have to take baby steps.

CRY

At the dawns first try
Igniting fiery islands adrift in the morning sky,
I heard the loon's cry.

For the next twenty five years
Through sunlight, rain, and tears,
I heard the loon's cry.

A sad bitter darkness will forever fill both my heart
and the dawn's first try
Because I was not there to hear the loon's final cry,
Goodbye.

Die

Sing a song of six pence, pocket full of rye
Do you go to heaven the minute you die?

Is there a time of waiting and doubt
Before it all gets sorted out.

You are you, both here and there
And knowing that your final outcome
will be just and fair.

All of the shoulda, woulda, coulda
done will not matter one bit
For it is what you did that counts when
on the judgment seat you sit.

Sing a song of six pence, pocket full of rye
Do you go to heaven the minute you die?

DRY

No matter how hard I grit my teeth trying not to cry
The bitter gruel of lonely has almost
squeezed my soul dry.

You open up your heart for one last time
because they care you were told
And then discarded like old trash
because you are now too old.

Old and alone is a miserable inhospitable place to be
Relegated to social oblivion by the mores of
an uncaring and self-centered society.

Keeping your honor intact by your standards keeping
Obligates you to forevermore all alone sleeping.

No matter how hard I grit my teeth trying not to cry
The bitter gruel of lonely has almost
squeezed my soul dry.

HERE

The first loon of the first spring alone, on the last
flight of the evening, calling for its mate without fear
And screaming as loud as I can, my soul wails
out, "Here Babe! Here! I'm Down Here!"

In a world of its own
With chicks to hatch, then feed until they are grown.

No matter how busy I try to be and with
unending prayer on bent knee
Beseeching so long and hard hoping, that the
anguish and pain will somehow turn my soul free

Time heals all wounds it is said.
But how does time heal a churning black hole
where your heart was, when on love was once fed.

The first loon of the first spring alone, on the last
flight of the evening, calling for its mate without fear
And screaming as loud as I can, my soul wails
out, "Here Babe! Here! I'm Down Here!"

HIT

Sitting all alone on the bench of the backyard fire pit
And the smell of scorched denim and the sting
of the embers when your skin they hit.

The heat burning through the knees
and legs of your pants
The ebb and surge of the fire as the breeze twists
the smoke into braided knots of quiet rants.

From untold eons in the past
Fire provided safety and warmth
from winter's freezing blast.

Uncountable eyes, mesmerized by the
flame's magic dance at night
Ignore the dance when the sun
provides the heat and light.

Sitting alone on the bench of the backyard fire pit
A d the smell of scorched denim and the sting
of the embers when your skin they hit.

MOON

Alone in what once was a home now
so cold, quiet, and dead.
And the moon turned red.

Whispering echoes of where once was
heard laughter love and joy
have now all fled.
And the moon turned red

Ages gone by and ages yet to come know
their moment then their moment is gone with
the setting sun when all light has fled
And the moon turned red.

These eyes will never again see this
creeping darkness bury Venus's lofty bed.
And the moon turned red.

Alone in what once was a home now
so cold, quiet, and dead.
And the moon turned red.

Hollow

When in the pain of your soul you, no longer wallow
The space becomes empty and your
soul becomes terribly hollow.

Like an empty house, without any light
The sound of empty follows your footsteps like
a jeering echo that now has wings and flight.

The sounds of love and laughter no
longer permeate the walls
And your spirit, in a deadly tailspin, falls.

You try to move on to another time and place
But because you are still alone, the endless
echoes haunt your soul's empty space.

When in the pain of your soul you, no longer wallow
The space becomes empty and your
soul becomes terribly hollow.

Straws

All alone still, just trying to survive
yet another day of lonely blahs
Even the slightest chance of ending the
bitter sound of yesterday's echoes
has me grasping at straws.

Relegated to obscurity by age and
society's oblivious whim
The chance of finding someone to love for
the fleeting time left to me is grim

The specter of lonely gleefully ignores
age, gender and color of skin
And with Satan's fiery fork he impales your heart with
searing hunger pangs that withers your soul from within.

All alone still, just trying to survive
yet another day of lonely blahs
Even the slightest chance of ending the
bitter sound of yesterday's echoes
has me grasping at straws.

Home

Gone at the crack of dawn so you can get
things done before the rest of the world wears
you down under the daily grindstone
And even when sheer exhaustion forces you to leave,
this is better than going back to a dark empty home.

A cold dark unlit house greets your weary eyes
And no matter how much you crave solace,
only the sounds of silence greet you and
the welcome is fraught with lies.

You push yourself to the bitter edge,
never stopping to eat or rest
Because if you don't, the pain and agony set
in and yet once again drags your soul through
the mire of yet another weary test.

Gone at the crack of dawn so you can get
things done before the rest of the world wears
you down under the daily grindstone
And even when sheer exhaustion forces you to leave,
this is better than going back to a dark empty home.

LATE

No matter how much I want to
open her love's garden gate
It won't count at all because I started
down her garden's path too late.

With her eyes already focused on someone
else further down the trail
No matter how deep and true my love for her
does not count because it is doomed to fail.

The light of her soul is a beacon flashing pulsar bright
But it never gets to me because I am in the
shadow of he that is already in her sight.

All of the dreams of a love so great and grand
Are but cobwebs torn asunder by his rush to get
the garden gate closed and tightly slammed.

No matter how much I want to
open her love's garden gate
It won't count at all because I started
down her garden's path too late.

Turning

A single season has come and gone as the sunlight
wanes, its rays are no longer burning
And my heart, like the leaves preparing
for winters cold, is turning.

Unlike the spring where there is hope for
rebirth and a chance at a new beginning
The coming of winter's bitter cold freezes your
soul in the icy clutch of loneliness demeaning.

The sour taste of fear and forever being alone
The desperate need for someone to love is like
a sin that for which you can never atone.

The sheer drudgery of eking out life day by dreary day
Banishes all hope of a life not in utter disarray.

A single season has come and gone as the sunlight
wanes, its rays are no longer burning
And my heart, like the leaves preparing
for winters cold, is turning.

Lights

Snow so cold: Snow so very white
and on those most bitter nights
Reflects the glory of the wondrous Northern Lights.

All of nature waits in the cradle of a winters sleep.
Knowing that the promise of a spring, then a summer
Is a promise that nature will keep.

When a loved one passes, the bitter cold of winter
grips your soul lost in the darkness so deep
But like the promise of nature, the return to a spring,
and then a summer is a promise our maker will keep.

Snow so cold: snow so very white.
and on those most bitter nights
Reflects the glory of the wondrous Northern Lights.

ME

No matter how much in my prayers I do plea
Why oh why is there not someone to love for me.

The gentle murmur of newlyweds married for 40 years
Holding hands as they support each other to
heaven's garden gate brings me to tears.

The gnawing grate of lonely hunger pangs
Rips at your heart like hungry rats with piranha fangs.

A recluse it would so easy to be
If the specter of alone would let just set me free.

No matter how much in my prayers I do plea
Why oh why is there not someone to love for me.

Pit

Yet another day my heart takes a nasty hit
And the only place I can try to find
any warmth is at the fire pit

In a place that is made for quiet conversation
just at dusk and into the night
Watching the flames do their age-old dance for
those who to love to watch it in delight.

No matter how you try to enjoy the flames as they play
There is no one there but you and
you have no words to say

Yet another day when my heart takes a nasty hit
And the only place I can try to find
any warmth is at the fire pit.

Punched

You work hard your entire life for those things in
the world of man that always gets you crunched
And then your world falls apart when
you get sucker punched.

All those things that money and time can buy
Utterly have no value when it is your
time from this world to fly.

To be tempered in the teaching of God
the Father and those ideals eternal
Means that on your knees you must repent and
smite from yourself those temptations infernal.

This is not ever a one-time task
If it is in the light of Christ's pure
love you want to humbly bask.

An eternal mate is the ultimate goal
If hand in hand through the gates of the
Celestial Kingdom you want to stroll.

You work hard your entire life for those things in
the world of man that always gets you crunched
And then your world falls apart when
you get sucker punched.

Toy

In every life there is something that creeps in
like a silent damp fog where there is no joy
And everything becomes like a broken toy.

You wind it up when you awake
And it scrabbles wounded across the floor
no matter how many times you wish it
would completely stop or really break.

Every day is drudgery of a to do list that never ends no
matter how hard you alone work and try And before bed
it is all you can do to not break down and silently cry.

The facade you wear allows you to keep it all inside
So no one sees the bitter sadness you truly must hide.

Lonely is a foul tasting condition
When every day, is the same twisted rendition.

You work all your life for the perfect
retirement of a golden summer day
And in reality, the goblins delight in taking it all away.

In every life there is something that creeps in
like a silent damp fog where there is no joy
And everything becomes like a broken toy.

Reign

There is pain where the tears fall like rain
And then there is pain where every part
of you aches and throbs
and torment has full reign.

Empathy and consolation in an empty
house is nowhere to be found
And a memory's faint echo is the only sound.

No healing touch or tender care
And this agonizing pain is almost too much to bear.

There is pain where the tears fall like rain
And then there is pain where every part
of part of you aches and throbs
and torment has full reign.

Shadows

When the light of your life is gone
And it takes every dig-down-deep gritty
bit of your strength to move on
You live with a soul full of shadows.

With no more joy, laughter and warm embraces
You have to cope with anguish, pain and left over traces.

You put on the false face of hope, trying to
mask the anguish of your loved one's death.
But on the inside your soul is cringing
with your every breath.

When the light of your life is gone
And it takes every dig-down-deep gritty
bit of your strength to move on
You live with a soul full of shadows.

Ring

Last night for the first since we married
I took off my wedding ring
So terribly afraid of guilt's, bitter sting.

It was the last word of the last line of the
last chapter of a now closed book
All of the words and the meaning between
the lines are now memories of the love we
shared and any future that death took.

It is time to stand in the light
And stand all amazed at the glory of the
beautiful soul that has now taken flight.

Life demands that we shun the darkness of despair
And let your heart be unafraid to see if there is
another heart that is also unafraid of a life to share.

No two hearts the same love share
Each is very different in the way they express
their love and their soul do bare.

Your soul has many rooms where
love can be carefully moored
And your heart has the only key to the
door where it is tenderly stored.

Last night for the first since we married
I took off my wedding ring
So terribly afraid of guilt's, bitter sting.

Sound

Green fire all around
A silent whisper the only sound.

Shafts of light, chasing night
Track an eagle's morning flight.

Rumble and grumble as only the tallest mountains can
They alone withstand the push of man.

When man is done and gone his way
Trees and mountains in their places stay.

Green fire all around
A silent whisper the only sound.

Terror

When the loss of the love of your life splinters
your soul like a shattered mirror
And much too soon comes the abject loneliness
that is your private hell, a prison of quiet terror.

The busy world around you swirls in colors
and sounds that blur into a meaningless
tasteless gruel of unending pain
The bowl that is your soul overflows with an
overpowering sense of loss and shame.

So very afraid that alone you will forever be
Because there is no one out there that will
have to your heart, the exactly right key.

The condemning guilt of searching
for a new life and love
Traps your heart in a prison of fear,
that bars the snow white dove.

When the loss of the love of your life splinters
your soul like a shattered mirror
And much too soon comes the abject loneliness
that is your private hell, a prison of quiet terror.

WINCE

When all the pain breaks down your
protective emotional fence
The bitter taste of despair makes you wince.

An unconscious mimic of the face of your soul
And unknowing expression of the hurt
that is making you pay the toll

The deep etches and lines on your face
Are created by the anguish and
pain of fears endless pace.

When all the pain breaks down your
protective emotional fence
The bitter taste of despair makes you wince.

Tanked

For reasons yet unknown at 10:47 a.m.
today my heart suddenly sank
Like those on the Titanic just before it tanked.

A massive pang of loss smacked me so very strong
That stopped me so dead cold that I needed
the help of a wall to walk along.

Something somewhere in my universe
got twisted and torn
And I know that when I get the sad news my
soul will wither yet again to be so forlorn.

For reasons yet unknown at 10:47 a.m.
today my heart suddenly sank
Like those on the Titanic when it tanked.

Tears

It is impossible to hold back the anguish, pain and fears
When your heart is full of frozen tears.

The terrible cold that chills you to the bone
When in the bed you now must sleep alone.

The unconscious reaching and touching for
someone that will never again be there
The cold empty space now wet with tears from the
endless searching of a frozen heart that will forever care.

It is impossible to hold back the anguish, pain and fears
When your heart is full of frozen tears.

Time

After losing the love of your life
and no further up the ladder of healing can you climb
Because you get stuck in time.

Even when the bitter anguish brought by
the horrific loss is sometimes gone
All of the memories flood in of the "what once was"
and welds you to the ladder rung you are standing on.

You would willingly sell your soul
To be back where there is light and
love in your life is the goal.

The seasons come and the seasons go
But there is no rhythm to the ebb and flow.
Because your heart is in the dark and does in a circle go.

After losing the love of your life
And no further up the ladder of healing can you climb
Because you get stuck in time.

STILL

Late at night is the hardest time,
neither awake nor asleep but
in the bitter dregs of the loneliest
part of anguish and pain
And in an unconscious act of
desperation, I still call her name.

At first I thought the loss and despair
would be the hardest of all
But the bitter cup of despair has a twin
sister that strips all of the flesh
from your heart and does not care about
how your soul shatters from the fall.

Try as you can and praying with all your might
Your soul gets so very weary of the daily dog fight.

No place to go, no place from where
the onslaught you can hide
When the most important part of
you has withered and died.

Late at night is the hardest time,
neither awake nor asleep but
in the bitter dregs of the loneliest
part of anguish and pain
And in an unconscious act of
desperation, I call her name still.

HOPE

Adagio

The music of a hauntingly beautiful song
And the music to a wonderful heart that I
will forever know, but never belong.
Adagio.

Trying to squeeze my heart into a place it could never fit
Hoping beyond hope that there would be
a tiny sliver of heart to myself knit.

The wondrous light that fills your soul when
the "I see you" connection is made
And the bitter sweet sorrows of understanding
that this amazing connection is not for me
and must quietly into a memory fade.

The music of a hauntingly beautiful song
And the music to a wonderful heart that I
will forever know, but will never belong.
Adagio.

Hope

When the loss of a loved one plunges your soul into the
bitter freezing cold and with despair you must cope
And when you get to the first spring
after this bitter winter, you hope.

When the sunshine floods your face with warmth and the
chance of a new beginning that only your soul will know
And like the first spring flower, new
petals unfurl and grow.

And when all of the love stored up in
your soul you can no longer hide
The tender shoots of a new life reaches for the
sun and all of your secret hopes do confide.

The hesitant reaching out of a wary and scarred soul
Looking though frightened eyes, at the chance
of a new life without being on despair's dole.

The flowers of spring need others like it for the
color and joy of an alpine meadow to bring
And when this magic happens, many souls
together in joy and love can sing.

When the loss of a loved one plunges your soul into the
bitter freezing cold and with despair you must cope
And when you get to the first spring
after this bitter winter, you hope.

Show

For the last chance of my life I pray for a woman that
could stand watch 200 miles offshore in a 100 knot blow
Spit fire at the wind and then every night pray
in earnest to God and in her life let it show.

Unafraid to take life head on no matter what the cost
Because of the way she lives her life on the road
to heaven's gate she is never, ever, lost.

To be willing to commit to forever with real intent
And during the sealing every word
promised is exactly what she meant.

The entire focus of my life will to love her like no other
And do whatever it takes be the husband that
that she would choose above all others.

To hold my soul to hers so very tight
So that when I pass on it will be her compass to my
love's pure light when it is her turn to take flight.

For the last chance of my life I pray for a woman that
could stand watch 200 miles offshore in a 100 knot blow
Spit fire at the wind and then every night pray
in earnest to God and in her life let it show.

Along

Tonight I listened to a wondrous soul-searching song
And then I finally understood that any chance
of a shared life was never there all along.

A true kindred spirit has danced on
another path her whole life long
Moving to the beat of her own soul's song.

So few times in the winding course of your life
Do you get the honor to truly know someone
who is unafraid to share their soul's strife.

"I see you" are not just words from a movie line
But the only way two souls can completely
merge into a single point of time.

The complete honesty mandated by such an exalted state
Fuses the joined thoughts into golden words
forever etched into your heart's eternal slate.

Tonight I listened to a wondrous soul-searching song
And finally I understood, that any chance of
a shared life was never there all along.

Alone

At a church dance made for singles trying to
meld hearts imprisoned by walls of stone
And is so very sad to watch those
who have to dance alone.

To be afraid to ask for a simple dance
that can lead to a celestial alter
When this is not the time to let your courage falter.

To relearn how to open your heart
Requires that you have the courage to meet
someone more than halfway to do your part.

At a dance made for singles trying to meld
hearts imprisoned by walls of stone
And is so very sad to watch those
who have to dance alone.

Back

Everything was so forlorn and black
And then I met you and got my celestial life back.

The joy, laughter, and song that I
had thought forever gone
Is what was hiding behind your eyes
when I saw your soul's song.

No longer is my life in retreat
And every morning your kiss will awake my greet

The songs that are sung in heaven in
honor of our Savior and Lord
Ensures that forever our souls are of one accord.

Everything was so forlorn and black
And then I met you and got my celestial life back.

Bring

Like all of the new butterflies of spring
You have to shed your chrysalis before into
a new life your heart you can bring.

The long cold of the winter of despair is
a fading memory that has to go
Before any chance of a new life you will ever know.

The chance of finding rainbows and
flying in the bright light of the sun
Totally depends on your heart's
willingness to grab life on the run.

There is not one moment to waste
If it is a brand new life you choose to live
and glory in the wondrous taste.

Like all of the new butterflies of spring
You have to shed your chrysalis before into
a new life your heart you can bring.

Climb

A different world and a different time
And very different mountains you must now climb.

The past is just that and only exists
in memories' siren song
And no matter how hard you try, going back is
but a dream where you do not now belong.

The good times are always the reason
to go to what once was
And your mind plays tricks on you with the
selected memories are the reason because.

Escape from the pain or age of the here and now
Guides your wish to brush the grey from
your hair and the furrows on your brow.

If wishes were horses we all could ride
Not a single good memory would find a place to hide.

A different world and a different time
And very different mountains you must now climb.

Breath

Fall is in full sway and all of nature is
grudgingly getting ready for their annual
brush with winter's temporary death
As the sun's life-giving rays grow cool in shorter days
and for the first time this morning I could see my breath.

Time has a way of wending through
your memories of loss and pain
And if your heart has healed enough to listen, gently
reminds you that there is nothing here left to gain.

Once bitter agonizing memories are now
seen as through frosted glass
And day by day the light behind the glass dims and
the terrible pain contained there fades from view as
your heart graduates into a very different class.

And with the passage of more time and space
The glass becomes opaque and dust covered except
where your forehead and hands mark the last time
you tried to peer into this dark terrible place.

Fall is in full sway and all of nature is
grudgingly getting ready for their annual
brush with winter's temporary death
As the sun's life-giving rays grow cool in shorter
days and for the first time this morning I could
see my breath.

Felicity

The tortuous scrabbling from the depths of despair
to the light utterly cannot be done alone as it
requires from those who care complete complicity
To the finding of your place in the bright light
of a shared amazing love and felicity.

The bitter dregs of time gone past
Fade from view as hand in hand with your
true love you forever hold fast.

All of the keys to the door of
heaven, both here and there
Are yours so long as the words of God in thought and
deed you daily prove you hear through honest prayer.

There will be tests of your faith that are promised
not to be beyond our strength to overcome
To prove to our Lord and Savior that we are worthy
of his presence when the on judgment day you
can rejoice that in His glorious light you meekly
bow to your brother, God's truly begotten Son.

The tortuous scrabbling from the depths of despair
to the light utterly cannot be done alone as it
requires from those who care complete complicity
To the finding of your place in the bright light
of a shared amazing love and felicity.

Bud

Words on a line and an image that
suddenly took your breath away
And your heart does a double thud
But before any relationship can bloom
there first has to be a bud.

The words that magically appear in
lines on a very small screen
But with your heart you must read between the lines
to decipher what the messages really do mean.

Fishing for understanding and for those
values that are in common shared
And the amazing discourses on so many different
things that defines those precepts that exactly
show how and why your heart cared.

Words on a line and an image that
suddenly took your breath away
And your heart does a double thud
But before any relationship can bloom
there fist has to be a bud.

For

Nothing is important at all at my
heart and soul's very core
Unless I have someone I love to do it for.

All those things both, large and small,
that true love does to you bring
That is exactly like having an unending supply of those
exquisite and rare flowers that only bloom in the spring.

Love is the rarest flower there ever will be
And must be nurtured and watered daily
with all your love so very tenderly.

There are tears that come with being
with the one you truly love
For it is tears of pure joy that waters those
rarest of flowers that fits around your
heart and soul like a silken glove.

Nothing is important at all at my
heart and soul's very core
Unless I have someone I love to do it for.

Fear

The first day of a brand new year
Left behind are the loss, pain and fear.

A fresh new start
Yours for the taking, if you choose to take part.

Dreams come in all colors, shapes and size
And to make yours come true takes vision, hard work
and luck before you get to claim the prize.

Dream big and dream high
For your only limit is the height of the sky.

The first day of a brand new year
Left behind are the loss, pain and fear.

CRY

Sing a song of sixpence, pocket full of rye
Every time we part, no matter what the reason
be, my heart worries and tries not to cry.

Until we get through the sealing's celestial gate
We are subject to the whims of an uncaring temporal
world and the evil of the adversary's hate.

Diligence to the words of God's
Prophets through the ages
Obligates that time and time again we read
with a prayerful heart the scripture's pages.

Sing a song of sixpence, pocket full of rye
Every time we part, no matter what the reason
be, my heart worries and tries not to cry.

Doubt

Minute by minute the days spool out
As you learn to survive heartache and doubt.

As your shared memories swirl around
you in the murky moat
You net only the good as they are the ones that highest
float and over time your net is filled with life and hope.

At that time from the murky water of despair
You emerge into bright sunshine with the
regrowth of life vibrating the air.

From your net, the memories once imprisoned by despair
Transform into exquisite butterflies that surround you
with color and light as they gently land on your wounded
heart that now can slowly relearn how to love and share.

Minute by minute the days spool out
As you learn to survive heartache and doubt.

Focus

In a world too busy of worldly things that makes
you so angry that you just want to scream and cuss
It is exactly at this point that you need
to remember not to lose your focus.

Those things that bring your venom and ire
Started out in Satan's fire

When your soul is in torment and in a dervish whirl
You need to get on your knees and
read passages from the Pearl.

Those things that really matter are not
the hot flashes of angers flame
But those things that a eternal soul does calm and tame.

In a world too busy of worldly things that makes
you so angry that you just want to scream and cuss
It is exactly at this point that you need to
remember not to lose your focus.

Heart

The aching impossible yearning of finding a kindred
soul willing to their soul with yours impart
When you have an uncommon heart.

When in the last inning of your life and
where every swing is a strike call
You hide your heart so very deep because the agony of
the swing makes your soul shatter into shards and fall.

The reality of ending your days completely alone
Creates a sense of hopelessness for a sin
you do not know how to atone.

The aching impossible yearning of finding a kindred
soul willing to their soul with yours impart
When you have an uncommon heart.

Keeper

Trying to find your perfect mate
is like fishing for the greatest catch of your
entire life that can be a sleeper
And when she decides that you are the one that
is for all time and eternity, you're her keeper.

When the light of Christ that is shining
from your soul is the bait
Your finding each other is not ever just luck or fate.

When you finally understand that there is a holy
reason and a plan from the very start of time
That in order to return to your heavenly home requires
an eternal mate that the alabaster stairs into the Celestial
Kingdom together, hand in hand, you will climb.

Trying to find your perfect mate
is like fishing for the greatest catch of
your entire life that can be a sleeper
And when she decides that you are the one that
is for all time and eternity, you're her keeper.

LIGHT

As hard you try and with all your might
It takes a very special soul to bring in the light.

The love of life surrounds them with a glow so bright
That you are in awe of the joy and the
light that is their soul's delight.

Would that everyone have this so very wonderful light
That the woes of the world would never
again be humanity's blight.

As hard you try and with all your might
It takes a very special soul to bring in the light.

It

There is an amazing perfect love waiting
for all if we will but trust our heart
enough to find the way to make it fit
It is like looking at the most beautiful rainbow
and cannot find the way to touch it.

The most perfect rainbow is Christ's pure
love and his forgiveness divine
And we but have to get on our knees in repentance to feel
the rainbow fill our heart and soul to the overflow line.

This kind of love is part and parcel of the
love you will find with an eternal mate
And it is not ever luck or fate but an eternal marriage
bound for heaven's Celestial rainbow gate.

There is an amazing perfect love waiting
for all if we will but trust our heart
enough to find the way to make it fit
It is like looking at the most beautiful rainbow
and cannot find the way to touch it.

Soon

When asked how long does it take true
love to sing its special tune
All your heart can hope for is soon.

When your whole world hangs by a single
thread of a soul trying to cope
All you can do is bare your soul and hope.

Forever is just a single word away
If you can get your true love to see
what your heart is trying to say.

"I love you" is not enough to get you to eternity's fate
For you must have faith in God's Celestial gate.

When asked how long does it take true
love to sing its special tune
All your heart can hope for is soon.

Paid

A crystal palace is never instantly made
And does not care about royalty, beauty,
or how much money you are paid.

It is not born in the white hot fire
of lust or passion driven
But starts as a small fragile crystal lattice inside the
souls of those that choose to their heart listen.

Each crystal lattice is the framework of the bridge
that connects two hearts at the very first look
As the love grows the fragile lattice becomes
a solid crystal that makes the cornerstone
of the risk at love they took.

Love is like a garden that must be carefully
tended every day and in every way
To nurture and grow the emotional crystals
needed to get the palace walls to grow and stay.

The sheer size of the palace is not the
measure of the love that built the wall
But rather, the perfect bonding of each carefully
placed crystal and how much pure light of love
shines from the souls that now live and grow inside
those connected crystal pillars that never will fall.

A crystal palace is never instantly made
And does not care about royalty, beauty,
or how much money you are paid.

Petals

The Tea Rose of China is the first flowering
bush of spring to ignore winter's barely
thawed grip of frozen soil like metal.
There are literally thousands of blooms that burst forth
and in but a few short days it starts raining petals.

Like pink snowflakes the petals from the
fading blooms cover the ground
And it occurred to me that these petals are
exactly like the days of our lives after they
bloomed and where the petals are found.

Each day of our lives has its own sets dreams
that try so very hard to bloom and like the
tea rose, it's many blossoms show
But unfulfilled dreams have no blossoms and the
withered buds, unopened, litter the ground.

Each new day brings its own set of buds that
try to bloom and its amazing blossoms show
And each one of us tries to as many
blooms as possible to grow.

It is very important to seek the blossoming
of your hopes and dreams sublime
Because if you do not, the dreams stop
and your life runs out of time.

The Tea Rose of China is the first flowering
bush of spring to ignore winter's barely
thawed grip of frozen soil like metal.
There are literally thousands of blooms that burst forth
and in but a few short days it starts raining petals.

Rainbow

Finding your eternal mate takes prayer
unending and faith from the beginning that
somewhere, somehow they will appear
And your heart will know the historic of gold is
really your one true love at the end of the rainbow.

The burden of a wounded heart makes
it a skeptical and cautious quarry
If you are the one that sees the hidden soul
shining so very bright and asking
for forever you cannot tarry.

An eternal mate is only found when holding
hands across the sealing room alter
And with a most sacred vow that forever
you will love and never, ever falter.

Knowing that never, ever, will you be alone
And that getting you and your family to the
Celestial Kingdom is the reason Christ surrendered
his soul on Calvary for your sins to atone.

Finding your eternal mate takes prayer
unending and faith from the beginning that
somewhere, somehow they will appear
And your heart will know the historic of gold is
really your one true love at the end of the rainbow.

Fears

After all this time of staying true through
a firestorm of pain and tears
And suddenly it is socially expected that you
find another love as soon as you can but your
soul freezes at the first word of what used to
be cheating and is now unfounded fears.

The very thought of looking is repugnant to
your established moral compass course
And your heart is now in the saddle
of a locoweed wild horse.

To fall is to get stomped to the point of death's gate
To stay means that you must learn to survive every
bone jarring twist that will decide your fate.

The fear of the unknown is like being
mesmerized by the nostrils flared
Of an evil Palouse that you must saddle and mount to
save your soul from being forever stomped and scared.

After all this time of staying true through
a firestorm of pain and tears
And suddenly it is socially expected that you
find another love as soon as you can but your
soul freezes at the first word of what used to
be cheating and is now unfounded fears.

PLAN

Things never go as they're supposed
to in the world of man
The hazard there in is that you cannot allow
it to change your eternal game plan

Life is the ultimate test of your strength and moral goal
For you dare not lose if Christ's pure
light you want more than a just a mole.

God will test your metal to get the right temper
Before the gate of the celestial kingdom you get to enter.

Things never go as they're supposed
to in the world of man
The hazard there in is that you cannot allow
it to change your eternal game plan.

Do

With every breath and heart beat I take
while she decides if my love will be forever true
My soul teeters on the knife edge of fate and my entire
future hangs in the balance of what she will decide to do.

She has the most exquisitely beautiful heart
For whom I would gladly sell my soul to
imbed my love into her precious heart and to
her eternal life be some important part.

The balance of life's trip must match
exactly to make it to heaven's gate.
And you cannot make to the very
top without a Celestial mate.

With every breath and heart beat I take
while she decides if my love will be forever true
My soul teeters on the knife edge of fate and my entire
future hangs in the balance of what she will decide to do.

JOY

Joy and Light

A small visit I had tonight
Brought into my life a ray of joy and light.

The words spoken were straight from the heart
An unpretentious understanding of common
emotions of life right from the start.

A wondrous smile in a house too long devoid of light
Provided a ray of hope that felt real, warm and right.

A small visit I had tonight
Brought into my life a ray of joy and light.

Hello

When it is my time through the veil to go
The last thing I want to see is you,
and feel your kiss hello.

When my spirit has gone to the other side for you to wait
It will be with unabated love I'll stand
patiently at heaven's gate.

God's gift of eternal life with an eternal wife
Is the grand prize of a mandated mortal life.

The Sealing Room alter is the key
to heaven's highest gate
Where, as here, new life for other worlds we can make.

The kiss hello is not just fate
For there is no "Goodbye" for an eternal mate.

When it is my time through the veil to go
The last thing I want to see is you,
and feel your kiss hello.

Arms

There is a special place of refuge that
I prize above all others and
It's in my wife's arms.

Without fail I fall asleep and
It's in my wife's arms.

When the entire day has been a real
bummer as I need solace and
It's in my wife's arms.

And there are those days that are
truly stellar I celebrate and
It's in my wife's arms.

As the days turn into years my daily fix of joy and
It's in my wife's arms.

When it's time for me to pass through the veil and
It's in my wife's arms.

Adore

Just when you think that your love for each
other could not grow stronger or more
There is a transition to a higher more rapturous realm
when you discover that "love" has become "adore".

As your souls intertwine and
interweave from the two to one
It is like the dawning of the new light that
comes with a glorious morning sun.

It is the path our Lord and Savior planned for all of
humanity so they could find their way back home
And paid for by His sinless sacrificial
death for our sins to atone.

Together heart to heart and hand in hand
We take ourselves and our family back to our pre-
mortal Celestial home in the Promised Land.

Just when you think that your love for each
other could not grow stronger or more
There is a transition to a higher more rapturous realm
when you discover that "love" has become "adore".

Soul

Like a freeze frame video shot of a winning goal
My world stopped mid breath as through
her eyes I saw her glorious soul

Never ever in my entire life has there been
such an instantaneous heart stopping rush
The grace that surrounded her soul so bright
squeezed my entire world in a love so strong
I thought my heart would crush.

Only once in a lifetime if God's love is so kind
She who was yours before, you now do find.

In a room so white, on your knees
basking in loves pure light
Can heaven on earth truly show to all love's real might.

Like a freeze frame video shot of a winning goal
My world stopped mid breath as through
her eyes I saw her glorious soul.

SNUGGLE

There are few tender mercies that can compete when
your mind is on the edge of sleep and all a muddle.
And then your eternal wife wriggles over
from her side of the bed and curls around
you in an all night long snuggle.

As she softly whisper snores with her
head and arm resting on your chest
Your heart and soul rejoice in the quiet moments that
demonstrate pure trust and eternal love at its very best.

The woes and worries of the day just melt away
When you truly understand that this amazing woman
will forever be with you standing through whatever
life brings and by your side will forever stay.

We must be tested over and over again
to purge our souls from sin
Before the doors of the Celestial Kingdom open
wide to let you and your eternal mate come in.

These eternal doors only open to those who
kneeled together at the Sealing Room alter
And with absolute single-minded purpose did not falter.

There are few tender mercies that can compete when
your mind is on the edge of sleep and all a muddle.
And then your eternal wife wriggles over
from her side of the bed and curls around
you in an all night long snuggle.

CHERISH

When all the other words of love have run
their course and in the doldrums perish
The word with all the love that holds
your heart enthralled is, cherish.

It is like the softest of silk threads
to surround your heart
Yet it is so strong that it is almost
impossible to break it apart.

It is the smell of the flowers of spring and the loam
that grew them for you with your true love to share
And states that forever and an eternity your
love to the Celestial Kingdom is the fare.

When all the other words of love have run
their course and in the doldrums perish
The word with all the love that holds
your heart enthralled is, cherish.

Forever

All the sonnets, songs and poems bespeak of love forever
but really means only while yet alive and still together.
But my love is a promise made while dressed all in white,
kneeling together in a temple committing to forever.

This is the real test of time
Where in the Celestial Kingdom the babies
we missed here become yours and mine.

The entire focus of my life will be
to love you like no other
And do whatever it takes to be the husband
that you would choose to our children mother.

All the sonnets, songs and poems bespeak of love forever
but really means only while yet alive and still together.
But my love is a promise made while dressed all in white,
kneeling together in a temple committing to forever.

BUSTLE

While sitting downstairs on the parlor
couch trying not to fidget or rustle
In the kitchen upstairs Easter dinner is being
made and the happy foot steps are all a bustle.

Sons coming out to join in the celebration's repast
So that as a family we can regale in those
stories, from a time gone past.

Time and space will soon make these
occasions harder and harder to do
And by grasping the moment now
makes those memories new.

Family time becomes fleeting moments as time goes by
And are so very precious in their mother's eye

While sitting on the parlor couch
trying not to fidget or rustle
In the kitchen upstairs Easter dinner is being
made and the happy foot steps are all a bustle.

DAY

When the impossible dream of finding someone
to love keeps your soul frozen and at bay
But by obeying the insistent prompting of the
Holy Ghost on both our souls created the most
amazing miracle of all, a temple wedding day.

Prayers will be answered if you have your soul
in the place to hear what the Savior says and shows
And then have the courage to follow the path
that your heart and soul now knows.

There is no greater treasure than
the gift of love unending
As was our Lord and Savior's plan
from the very beginning.

Holy covenants made to each other with
love's pure light and holy duty
Open the door to the Celestial
Kingdom's unending beauty.

When the impossible dream of finding someone
to love keeps your soul frozen and at bay
And by obeying the insistent prompting of the
Holy Ghost on both our souls created the most
amazing miracle of all, a temple wedding day.

Blush

The sun just touching the top of Pioneer
Peak with a quiet pink kiss of hush
Just like a young girl's first kiss makes her
face turn pink with her first blush.

A new dawn on a clear blue Sunday morn
And to church you go to be like the mountain
and in God's infinite love, reborn.

Toiling the entire night through
To ensure that with tools put down so the
dawn's first light would be in view.

The sun just touching the top of Pioneer
Peak with a quiet pink kiss of hush
Just like a young girl's first kiss makes
her face pink with her first blush.

GRACE

When waltzing through life with
heaven's most beautiful face
Like the Viennese Waltz it is done
with the most amazing grace.

The love that shines from her soul through her eyes
Lights up my soul just like heaven's
fire across the Northern skies.

Like Katrina and Helmut's 50 years of waltzing
heart to heart in the Schonbrunn Palace Grand
Ballroom with their love guiding their feet
Their obvious love for each other drops your
jaw in utter awe of their glorious feat.

When waltzing through life with
heaven's most beautiful face
Like the Viennese Waltz it is done
with the most amazing grace.

Endearment

It's not the big things that a marriage does make,
but the small quiet time conversations that can be no
more than a peck or an eyebrow lift to ask and answer
those important questions like how your day went
Because those quiet or unspoken words go
directly to the heart and soul and are the
most important terms of endearment.

The words spoken during your nightly prayers
kneeling together with your eternal mate
Are like threads of the strongest silk that weave
a tapestry that binds you together ensuring the
entry through Celestial Kingdom's gate.

Words are not mere trifles as they have
immense power and weight
And should never be used when, anger generates
the pestilence of bitterness or hate.

You absolutely have the power and will to
use those words that love a heart can fill
And Satan will if given the chance,
deluge your mind and mouth with swill.

It's not the big things that a marriage does make,
but the small quiet time conversations that can be no
more than a peck or eyebrow lift to ask and answer
those important questions like how your day went
Because those quiet or unspoken words go
directly to the heart and soul and are the
most important terms of endearment.

Grateful

As I held my Lady enfolded in my arms tonight
as we said our evening prayers faithful
I did not forget to tell her how much I loved
her and would be forever eternally grateful.

The reason we are here is to prove worthy
to return to our pre-mortal home
That is so important that our Lord and
Savior had to die for us to atone.

The choices made day by day are like stepping
stones across a murky evil stream
And it requires a temple marriage to the love
of your life to achieve the celestial dream.

As I held my Lady enfolded in my arms tonight
as we said our evening prayers faithful
I did not forget to tell her how much I loved
her and would be forever eternally grateful.

Miles

Wrap the glory of a sunrise into the sparkle in her eyes,
the brightness of a noonday sun into her smiles
Combine this with the grace that shines from her soul
Just to see my love I would crawl on
shards of glass for miles.

To love and be loved is the grand prize of this mortal
life for which we must suffer pain, sorrow and strife
For the losing the one you love cuts
far deeper than any knife.

Like a teenager on his very first date,
Stuttering and stammering trying to find the
just right words that will decide my fate.

Wrap the glory of a sunrise into the sparkle in her eyes,
the brightness of a noonday sun into her smiles
Combine this with the grace that shines from her soul
Just to see my love I would crawl on
shards of glass for miles.

HER

A winter's night after the snow fell as
soft and quiet as a lovers whisper
And the night so very still that Mother Earth's
night time lover the stars, leaned down one
by one, and so very tenderly, kissed her.

A rare hush fill the entire sky with as if
it was wrapped in starlit cotton
And so very quiet you can hear your soul
gently reminding your heart that nights
like this will not soon be forgotten.

And a barely moving breeze now completely stopped
like the frozen hands of a broken alarm clock
As the quiet thumps of the snow clumps leaving
the branches softly bouncing as a backwards
chime in a left handed grandfather clock.

Like all lovers, the fickle stars will leave in
order to hide from the returning sunrise
Only to return every night and on those special nights,
the Northern Lights flitter from star to star trying
to generate for us a once in a lifetime surprise.

A winter's night after the snow fell as
soft and quiet as a lovers whisper
And the night so very still that Mother Earth's
night time lover the stars, leaned down one
by one, and so very tenderly, kissed her.

Honor

It does not take long at all to understand that
every one of your children have their own cadence
and beat that can be quiet or very loud and every
once in a while they do something that makes you
as a parent so very proud and in the very next
instant they say something that just makes you
fill their mouth with a bar of soap to launder
And finally at some point in time you truly
understand that God has entrusted their childhood to
you and watching them grow has been your honor.

Just like you they have their free
agency to use as they see fit
And sometimes all you can do is love them
unconditionally; just as God the Father
does for all his children's benefit.

The hardest lesson a parent must learn
is to truly understand that it not your
words that they pay attention to
But every deed and action is truly what they
so carefully watch and in fact do as you do.

With that foremost understanding
in your prayers and mind
You must walk the walk if the Lord
and Savior you want them to find.

It does not take long at all to understand that
every one of your children have their own cadence
and beat that can be quiet or very loud and every
once in a while they do something that makes
you as a parent so very proud and in the next
instant they say something that just makes you
fill their mouth with a bar of soap to launder
And finally at some point in time you truly
understand that God has entrusted their childhood to
you and watching them grow has been your honor.

Intimate

When through the eyes of my soul I can see your
soul flash the colors of your true love pulsate
My soul rejoices in tears and song that are
only heard by our hearts intimate.

Celestial love can only be forever meant
If you choose every second of forever together spent.

It is as close as two souls can ever be
When intertwined and sewn together with the
blessing of Christ's pure love that on the cross he
died to insure redemption for all of humanity.

It is not a word of mere trifles for an act without
the commitment of husband and wife
But the exact nature of how true love between
husband and wife should be for their eternal life.

When through the eyes of my soul I can see your
soul flash the colors of your true love pulsate
My soul rejoices in tears and song that are
only heard by our hearts intimate.

ONE

With a billion souls to search through for a mate that
has a soul as pure and beautiful as the morning sun.
And with the commitment of literally forever,
for me there can be and I found, the only one.

And with the help of Christ's perfect
love in which we bask
Like the most intricate puzzle, the pieces have to mesh
perfectly if together forever is the goal and task.

As the pieces of our soul mesh and
into one soul meld forever
God's plan of heaven, both here on earth and
in the Celestial Kingdom there is where
we shall reside together.

With a billion souls to search through for a mate that
has a soul as pure and beautiful as the morning sun.
And with the commitment of literally forever,
for me there can be and I found, the only one.

Groans

It seems only but yesterday that my heart and soul
would forever stand on an empty dance floor so all alone
Then the miracle of God's gift of eternal love
shattered the walls of stone that entombed my soul to
a fate uttered by the loneliest of desperate groans.

When a promise made amid the brightest of light
Came true in a poem that carried my
soul to my hearts delight

Words written in haste while the tears were flowing
Allowed my soul to embed my love in a way
that she who already knew that my heart
and soul were only for her showing

It seems only but yesterday that my heart and soul
would forever stand on an empty dance floor so all alone
Then the miracle of God's gift of eternal love
shattered the walls of stone that entombed my soul to
a fate uttered by the loneliest of desperate groans.

Longer

Every day our love grows stronger
grows by leaps as our souls meld
And the intertwining of our souls heals all the
pain and wounds as our hearts are weld.

Just when you think that the emotions
could not bring loves pure light to the
darkest coldest corners of your soul
You finally understand that this love is part and
parcel of our Lord and Savior's heavenly goal.

Every day our love grows stronger
grows by leaps as our souls meld
And the intertwining of our souls heals all the
pain and wounds as our hearts are weld.

CRADLE

One of the tender mercies that comes with
an eternal mate, is a love so great that it
is measured with a golden ladle
And in those moments so tender, that
in your arms you do her cradle.

The harried pace of life too busy it is easy to forget
the who and why together you are
And it is so important to take the time to daily
remind her that heaven's gate is not that far

All it takes is a quiet moment alone to peer through
her eyes to her wondrous soul forever new
To know that she has devoted her forever to you.

Our time here is measured moment
to moment unknown infernal
So it is critical that every moment counts
for memories that are eternal.

One of the tender mercies that comes with
an eternal mate is a love so great that it
is measured with a golden ladle
And in those moments so tender, that
in your arms you do her cradle.

Momma

My lady so fine and fair came over to help put
away the winter wood supply to keep us warm
and had never ridden a 6-wheeler Brahma
Showing her how to run the bike through the
back yard park and little did I know that I was
making a wild hotrod 6-Wheeler Momma.

The first time around the high trail loop she made
many clangs as the snowplow grew new dents
And the trees along trailside got bent as
around and around the loop she went.

After a few practice runs the clanging stopped and the
confidence and skill went beyond her wildest dreaming
And the fun began as she wound it up faster on every
run until on the downhill side, standing up, with her
hair streaming in the wind, sporting an ear-to-ear
grin, she came down the trail just flat out screaming.

My lady so fine and fair came over to help put
away the winter wood supply to keep us warm
and had never ridden a 6-wheeler Brahma
Showing her how to run the bike through the
back yard park little did I know that I was
making a wild hotrod 6-Wheeler Momma.

Be

A most important tenant of our religious
conviction is the faith you can marry your
soul mate for all time and eternity
And with that most sacred of vows forever embedded
in my soul, my wife will be the last person here I see,
and when she passes through the veil I will be the
person there my now eternal wife for me will be.

All of the memories we make here are
indelibly woven in the fabric of your soul
So that as those precepts learned here and the work
that needs to be done there to teach those who have
already passed through the veil will allow our faith and
love to grow by leaps and bounds is the Master's goal.

The love for each other we have here now is as
but child's play because the love shared there are
mirrors of the pure love of our Savior's glow
And we will absolutely understand because face to face
with our Lord and Savior's grace and love we will know.

A most important tenant of our religious
conviction is the faith you can marry your
soul mate for all time and eternity
And with that most sacred of vows forever embedded
in my soul, my wife will be the last person here I see,
and when she passes through the veil, I will be the
person there my now eternal wife for me will be.

WAVE

Finding the perfect love is like trying to cross
an ocean in order for your soul to save
The seas can be calm and flat as glass or the wind can
just scream through the rigging with the seas slamming
the wheelhouse glass, but there is nothing, absolutely
nothing that can prepare you for the rogue wave.

A rouge wave can come in a flat, calm sea or
during a howling storm with fifty-foot seas
Like Thor's Hammer it will smash everything
on deck, roll the hull to the rail and in pure panic
take you in repentance and fear to your knees.

Ordinary life can have rouge waves exactly the same way
From out of nowhere they can smash your
entire life all asunder any time night or day.

But the only way that your eternal soul can
be saved, no matter what happens here
Is to take Christ's pure love, and the repentance that He
does give to those that to their heart they hold Him near.

Finding the perfect love is like trying to cross
an ocean in order for your soul to save
The seas can be calm and flat as glass or the wind can
just scream through the rigging with the seas slamming
the wheelhouse glass, but there is nothing, absolutely
nothing that can prepare you for the rogue wave.

LAND

Love is like a precious crystal that just magically
appears in your heart's hand And can be
totally unplanned as it thaws the landscape
of your heart's frozen and barren land.

Like tiny spotlights, the light from the facets
of the crystal allows you see the strength of
your love grow and even though your hands are
tightly cupped it shines all the way through your
hands with your entire heart's love light glow
This amazing light guides you and your
eternal mate to the sealing room alter and
will forever together as one family grow.

Love is like a precious crystal that just magically
appears in your heart's hand And can be
totally unplanned as it thaws the landscape
of your heart's frozen and barren land.

Shangri-La

A house is just a house no matter how lavish or la-di-da
It takes love of God's pure light that shines
from the souls of those you love to make it
Shangri-La.

Whether a castle with spires that reach the
sky or a humble abode that barely gets by
It's the love that is stored inside that makes it
a home that day or night lights up the sky.

Those riches created by the whim of the natural man
Are not, and never will be part of God's eternal plan.

The arduous dangerous journey back
home to our heavenly host
Require faith, prayer, works, and repentance to
our Lord and Savior who knowingly and willingly
forfeited his life so we could hear the quiet
words of forgiveness from the Holy Ghost.

A house is just a house no matter how lavish or la-di-da
It takes love of God's pure light that shines
from the souls of those you love to make it
Shangri-La.

Overlook

A true angel with a soul so shiny and
bright that my breath it took
Abandoned and left alone for far too long and
a perfect love that I could not overlook.

Never ever in a lifetime almost
Have I found a temple worthy soul that
listened to a primary song and chose for
me to honor my undying love's boast.

Sitting on a boulder beside a river rushing so fast
That even above the roar she heard my plea to take
her to the temple and marry for an eternity ever last.

Her soul is a guiding light to all that she does know
And with great impatience to the sealing alter
I beseech a merciful God to let us go.

A true angel with a soul so shiny and
bright that my breath it took
Abandoned and left alone for far too long and
a perfect love that I could not overlook.

QUILTING

True love is learning how to take the patchwork that
is your soul that can take love's heat without wilting
And piece by piece the patches are sewn
together exactly like quilting.

From the many pieces a single purpose of an
eternal life together is stitch by stitch hand sewn
That will allow you to honor God the
Father at his very throne.

The strength of fabric and stitches is a
direct result of the shared following of your
faith to the temple to do God's work
For there is never a moment to lose to ensure
that you never, ever, your calling shirk.

The quilt made here by your family eternal
Is but a square in the quilt made by
your heavenly mother maternal.

True love is learning how to take the patchwork that
is your soul that can take love's heat without wilting
And piece by piece the patches are sewn
together exactly like quilting.

Prince

There is a children's story about a nobleman hexed by an
evil witch to wear the guise of a frog forever hence
And I truly understand the predicament the frog was
in because this was how I felt until I was kissed by my
princess so fair that from a frog I became her prince.

Abject loneliness is very close to an evil hex that you
cannot avoid
As your heart and soul yearn for the perfect love
to fill to overflowing a bitter cold empty void.

Yearning and trust do not go hand in hand
Because after being burned or scorned you wear
on your heart a terrible fear like a cattle brand.

Holding your honor clean and pure
Allows the spirit to do his wondrous work of matching
you with a mate that allows the gates of heaven bid open
if you but honor God and to the end together endure.

Every honorable man is a prince in his own special way
And only needs to remain true to find the
perfect princess to with pure love to sway.

There is a children's story about a nobleman hexed by
and evil witch to wear the guise of a frog forever hence
And I truly understand the predicament the frog was
in because this was how I felt until I was kissed by my
princess so fair that from a frog I became her prince.

It

We all have those special places that house amazing
memories that still bring tears of joy to your heart
and soul as a single instantaneous composite
For me one of my most important memories is
where on a river boulder I proposed to my now
eternal mate, where a river runs through it.

You can live almost an entire married lifetime
and be at the end utterly all alone
Because the marriage cannot follow after you pass
through death's portal and your heart is as a stone.

Only those mates worthy of a temple sealing
Can rejoice that death is but the door to heavens highest
kingdom where your mate will join you as together you
honor God's plan of salvation face to face kneeling.

Only those that in utter righteousness use the iron
rod of God as their compass to heavens highest gate
But can only do so enter hand in
hand with their eternal mate.

We all have those special places that house amazing
memories that still bring tears of joy to your heart
and soul as a single instantaneous composite
For me one of my most important memories is
where on a river boulder I proposed to my now
eternal mate, where a river runs through it.

Mist

A woman with eyes shining with a special
glow from being passionately kissed
Add a gentle breath on the back of her
neck and on her skin is a lover's mist.

Passion's fire still yet held in by honors code
And day by day the trip to eternity does unfold.

A woman with eyes shining with a special
glow from being passionately kissed
Add a gentle breath on the back of her
neck and on her skin is a lover's mist.

Rose

Flowers have a way of directly conversing
with your soul through your eyes and nose
But the only flower that evokes the
passions of love is the ruby red rose.

Flowers are so very precious as they delight
the heart and soul in so many ways
Because their beauty is measured in the
heartbeats of a few short days.

As a child frolicking in a meadow full of
wildflowers almost as tall as your head
And the smell of the blossoms fills the room
from the clothes you removed to go to bed.

The childhood memories long past and
those many memories yet to be made
And if you choose, flowers can be the notes
of the many songs that can and should
through the eyes of your soul be played.

Flowers have a way of directly conversing
with your soul through your eyes and nose
But the only flower that evokes the
passions of love is the ruby red rose.

On

When you open up your heart one last
time, putting aside the prison of fear and
pain where your soul had gone
And my amazing Lady wraps her arms around
my neck, looks through my eyes into my very
soul and softly proclaims, "Bring it on."

When the fears of the difference of our years
brings those things that age makes you don
And yet again she wraps her arms around my
neck, looks through my eyes into my very
soul and softly proclaims, "Bring it on."

The fire of passion that burns so very bright
Is but a reflection of our Lord and Savior's
redeeming pure love and light.

Covenants about to be made while kneeling at
the sealing room alter dressed all in white
Ensures that we will reside forever in the Celestial
Kingdom's palaces made from love's pure light.

When you open up your heart one last
time, putting aside the prison of fear and
pain where your soul had gone
And my amazing Lady wraps her arms around
my neck, looks through my eyes into my very
soul and softly proclaims, "Bring it on."

Sent

I asked for her pillow so that while I slept, on
my soul her scent I could indelibly imprint
But the most amazing thing happened last night as I
slept; my soul remembered her aroma from before and
realized that for me she was literally, heaven sent.

To most this is but an idyllic boast
But to those that understand the real path to here
also know that we all came from a heavenly host.

As our now conjoined souls relearned how to speak
to each other without the need for the spoken word
The true meaning of eternal love has forged a bond
that shouts "Glory unto God" that in the hallowed
halls of the celestial kingdom is clearly heard.

I asked for her pillow so that while I slept, on
my soul her scent I could indelibly imprint
But the most amazing thing happened last night as I
slept; my soul remembered her aroma from before and
realized that for me she was literally, heaven sent.

SNORE

While holding my lady in my arms making
the plans for us and our future in store
She curled up on the couch and with her head
on my lap did quietly start to snore.

Trusting as a child trusts the ones they love
Her snoring is as gentle and not
unlike the cooing of a dove.

Would that I could but join her in that sweet song
But until we are temple sealed, apart we must belong.

While holding my lady in my arms making
the plans for us and our future in store
She curled up on the couch and with her head
on my lap did quietly start to snore.

Tumultuous

Falling in love is not for the weak for it is almost never
anything but a firestorm of emotions spontaneous
And your whole heart whirls around and around like a
leaf trapped in a hurricane of emotions tumultuous.

There can be a firestorm of white hot
flame of spontaneous combustion
Or the sureness that comes when prayers are
answered by listening to the still small voice that
calms the sea of doubts and storms of frustration.

True love comes not as Kilauea shooting
molten lava a mile high into the sky
But the pure light of love that makes a holy
beacon of tempered passion until on your knees
and holding hands on the sealing room alter
where as eternal husband and wife the tears of
love fills your heart and then together you cry.

Falling in love is not for the weak for it is almost never
anything but a firestorm of emotions spontaneous
And your whole heart whirls around and around like a
leaf trapped in a hurricane of emotions tumultuous.

Tracks

As I revel in the giggles and joyful screaming of
the grandchildren as they plummeted down the
sled hill, sometimes on the sled or on their backs
It occurred to me that the only sign left after
they are gone is in the snow, their tracks.

In a very short time the snow will
have given way to spring
And the only way back are those things
that your memory does bring.

One way or another we all leave a trail or track
But in reality it is a one-way trip, for
there is truly but one way back.

Every path we take leads us to another thought or place
And the decision is always whether to
stay in the rut you have put yourself in or
stand tall and your shoulders brace.

Life was never designed to be right or fair
But is the ultimate test of how to get from here to there.

Our Lord and Savior requires that we be
tempered to withstand evil's wily power
Before we get to pass through the gates of
the Celestial Kingdoms tallest tower.

The tracks we leave are not in the mortal realm here
But in your souls indelible memory of
everything you did or hold dear.

As I revel in the giggles and joyful screaming of
the grandchildren as they plummeted down the
sled hill, sometimes on the sled or on their backs
It occurred to me that the only sign left after
they are gone is in the snow, their tracks.

SUNSHINE

Light can be like magic when it illuminates
by grace from my perfect Lady so fine
Her glow can be soft and silken or fiery passion driven
but above all else she is my life-giving sunshine.

In a world so long dark and a bitter cold
that freezes your soul into solid ice
The warmth of her smile and the light from her
eyes is like a miraculous spring that once was beyond
all hope of a winning roll with loaded dice.

Spring's warmth into summer is still
just over the horizon of love yet to be found
But the glory of that which could be
keeps my soul like the top,
spinning round and round.

Light can be like magic when it illuminates
by grace from my perfect Lady so fine
Her glow can be soft and silken or fiery passion driven
but above all else she is my life-giving sunshine.